Squirrelly Sally

by Doreen (Claiborne) Ingram

Illustrations by Mark Ingram

Other Books by Doreen Ingram

My Sanctuary
Keepers of the Wild
The Mission

Copyright 2019
All rights reserved—Doreen (Claiborne) Ingram
First Edition

Cover and interior design by J.K. Eckert & Company, Inc.

All rights reserved. No part of this publication may be reproduced or transmitted in any form or by any means, including photocopying, recording, or other electronic or mechanical methods, without the prior written permission of the publisher, except in the case of brief quotations embodied in critical reviews and certain noncommercial uses permitted by copyright laws.

SUSANNA LAGOON™ Books
An imprint of J. K. Eckert and Company, Inc.
Nokomis, FL 34275

www.doreeningram.com

ISBN: 978-0-9915252-6-3

Dedication

The Wildlife Sanctuary of Northwest Florida has a special place in my heart. They are fantastic, animal-lovin' people who work endlessly to help wildlife. The sanctuary is a nonprofit organization, working to provide appropriate care for injured or orphaned indigenous wildlife; their objective is rehabilitation and release, seven days per week. This book is also dedicated to all of the people in this world who care for, rescue, rehabilitate and release, or house, if needed, animals that would have perished if not for their love, care, and hard work.

Thank you, John Ingram, for making the numerous release and rehabilitation cages I needed that allowed me to properly care for wildlife and other animals until their release. Over the years, he has built many squirrel and flying squirrel nesting boxes and the one Sally lived in for a few years!

My three children—Melissa, Thomas, and Daniel—have always been such a great help when it came to assisting me with some of the age-appropriate chores I needed help with while fostering animals. Observing me care for the animals that I fostered for a nearby wildlife sanctuary taught my children so much about animals and their behavior, all the while bringing empathy for living creatures. I have three loving, caring, and empathic children whom I adore! My son Daniel is studying to become a veterinarian.

My brother-in-law, Mark Ingram, did such a wonderful job helping me with this book through his beautiful and imaginative illustrations. His volunteer work helped me to be able to finish this book and add it to the three others I have already published. For someone who had never done illustrations for a book before, you did an amazing job, so thank you very much!

Thank you so much for your support and purchases of my books.

Contents

Preface vii

Chapter 1. Sally 1

Chapter 2. Growth Means Change 7

Chapter 3. Big Day Outside 12

Chapter 4. An Emotional Moment 18

Chapter 5. Time to Go 22

Chapter 6. Spring and New Life 32

Chapter 7. A Special Call for Help 36

Chapter 8. Age Takes a Toll 41

About the Author 50

The Illustrator 51

Photos 52

PREFACE

Sally was just one of the hundreds of squirrels and other small wildlife I have fostered and released for a wildlife sanctuary in my hometown. But…Sally was precious to me and extraordinary, and that is putting it lightly!

Sally taught me, my children, and all the children *and* adults who had the pleasure of making her acquaintance, how much a small life, full of personality and energy, could be such a joy and aid in bringing empathy for this a fairly common and sometimes loathed animal. SQUIRRELS!

Sally was an icon in my yard, a favorite of all my family and friends. She lived in the woods nearby until an injury and temporary disappearance provoked me to ask for a squirrel house to be built for her. John gladly built her a house and hung it high in a nearby tree. That was her home for a few years, and she raised at least one litter of pups (baby squirrels) in it until a stronger-willed squirrel booted her out. I knew that being FREE was the most important and humane thing I could do for Sally. I prayed for her safety and her wisdom, and that each day she would stay alert and watch out for the hawks, owls, snakes, cats, and other predators. She will forever be in my heart, and I loved her very much.

1

Sally

Who could have imagined that a tiny, pink, newborn squirrel would make such a huge difference in so many lives? Her name was Sally, and it was a miracle she survived the fall from an immense and towering oak tree…the fall that would bring her deep into the lives of a family who would never be the same after that fateful day.

She was born in a very sturdy nest made of leaves and sticks, way up in the topmost part of an oak tree. The nest was built single-handedly by her mother. Her father played no part in building the nest, or in feeding and rearing Sally and her siblings. It is the nature of all squirrels that the mothers do these jobs alone. The fathers don't share this big responsibility, which is a behavior unlike some other nest-building animals such as birds.

Sally probably had one or two siblings, but we will never know the details of her life before the fall. Perhaps her nest was destroyed by a windstorm and she fell to the ground, or maybe she was accidentally pushed out of her warm and cozy home. It makes no difference how it happened; it was her fate.

Her eyes were still closed when she landed on the cold, hard ground, and she had no fur at all because she was only a few days old. That's how squirrel babies begin their lives—blind and bald. Lucky for her, it was autumn and there were layers of dead leaves beginning to build up on the ground. The leaves served as a slight cushion to break her fall. Squirrels are supposed to stay in their nests until they're old enough to learn to climb and are all furred out. Poor Sally wouldn't get to grow up with her siblings and be taught how to find nuts, berries, and new young tender leaves to eat. She would never watch her mother gather acorns, seeds, and nuts, and then bury them in the soil so they could be located and eaten at a later date. Squirrels dig shallow holes, drop in the seeds and nuts from their mouths, and then lightly cover them up with dirt and leaves or twigs. This is done so that another nosey squirrel might not find them. Even after months, the squirrels can remember where more than half of their treasure was hidden so they can eat it when there is less food to forage for. Nor would Sally have the opportunity to observe her mother dig for young root bulbs to eat. She wouldn't get to do any of these things, but luckily for her, a little girl was examining a ladybug in her large backyard where the oak tree grew and found Sally—just a tiny, pink baby alone on the ground. With gentle and warm hands, the girl lifted the squirrel close to her chest and walked ever so slowly into her home, so as not to scare the baby further.

Who was the little girl, you might ask? She was a quiet and very shy child, the sort of child you might not even notice in a classroom full of twenty other first-graders. She was a small-framed girl with a big heart and a beautiful smile. Her long, straight hair was usually pulled back into a ponytail and was dark blond in color. Her big brown eyes held a look of innocence but also of fear. This little girl was much more at ease in the presence of animals than people. She was a bright and an agreeable child and got along fine with the other children. Her name was Melissa.

The newborn squirrel was not the first animal Melissa had brought home to Mommy, and it would not be the last.

Baby birds, injured birds, stray cats, a couple of dogs, lizards, frogs, tadpoles from a nearby pond, and just about anything else that could crawl came through the door and entered her home…though maybe only for a minute or two! Mommy had to put her

foot down sometimes and send Melissa back outside to release the unwelcome guest. Some of the critters Melissa brought home, like injured or baby birds, were promptly taken to the area wildlife sanctuary for professionals to care for and hopefully release at the right time.

One time, Melissa thought it would be fun to bring a jar full of ants into her room and watch them tunnel through the dirt like they did in the ant farm her teacher had in the classroom at her school. Melissa thought she had better poke some holes in the jar lid so the ants could breathe. The next morning, Mommy, with bare feet, came into the room to wake Melissa for school. Suddenly she felt red-hot stings on her feet! She discovered that the ants had left the jar and were crawling all over the floor. But these weren't just any old ants; they were fire ants that Melissa had retrieved from a mound in the neighbor's yard the day before!

Mommy had been a nurse for years, and she had considerable medical knowledge and past experience with wildlife, and her patience with her daughter was never-ending. She knew that one day Melissa would come out of her shell, so to speak, and that her deep love and respect for animals would come to make a difference in her own life, and possibly even in others.

§ § § § §

"Mommy!" Melissa cried out as soon as she opened and carefully entered the front door. "Mommy! Come quick! It's alive but it needs our help.

Luckily for tiny Sally, Mommy knew just what to do. Sally wasn't much bigger than a child's thumb, and she was far too cool to the touch to survive much longer. Normally, a baby squirrel would be nice and warm cuddled up to its soft, furry mother. But since Sally had lost her home and her mother, a heating pad would do the trick. Mommy put Sally into a  small box with a soft baby blanket that she borrowed from Melissa's doll bed. Then she put the box, with Sally in it, on top of the heating pad, which was set to a low and constant heat.

While Sally warmed up inside the box, Mommy got to work warming some special milk. Melissa wondered why Sally couldn't drink the same kind of milk she did. Mommy told her that it would upset the baby squirrel's tummy. Squirrels need a different formula than humans in order to grow into a healthy and happy adult squirrels.

Mommy said they would keep the little squirrel just until she was old enough to make it on her own in the wild, when she could find food for herself. That was not what Melissa was hoping for; she wanted to keep the squirrel she had carried home for her own.

"Honey, this baby needs us now," Mommy said. "But one day, it will want to live in the woods and climb trees and leap from branch to branch and be wild. It just wouldn't be fair to keep something with that much energy and life inside a cage. I will make a deal with you. You give her a name and after we release her in a few months, we can call her for some treats now and then. If she comes back for the treats…that will be her choice." Melissa agreed, and that is how the oh-so-tiny, pink baby squirrel got her name…Sally.

2

Growth Means Change

Though little girls grow very fast, baby squirrels grow even faster. Within a few weeks, Sally was three times the size she was when she was found and had very fine, soft fur covering her body. She was a light grey color, and though the fur was short and fine, it wouldn't take long before she would have a lot more and her tail would begin to get bushy and long. Her eyes were still shut, and there was no way to rush them open.

Nature would take care of that when the time was right.

Each morning now, Melissa woke up thirty minutes early to watch Mommy prepare the special milk formula for Sally. She had watched Mommy feed all kinds of baby animals many times, and on occasion, she got to help under Mommy's supervision. She checked it to make sure it wasn't too hot, and then she fed Sally and cleaned her mouth just right so as not to let the milk cause irritation on her skin.

At first, Sally needed to be fed every two to three hours, and Mommy had to wake up twice each night to feed her. Raising Sally took time and effort, but she was growing, eating well, and seemed right at home on her little pink and red flowered blanket, waking up only long enough for each meal.

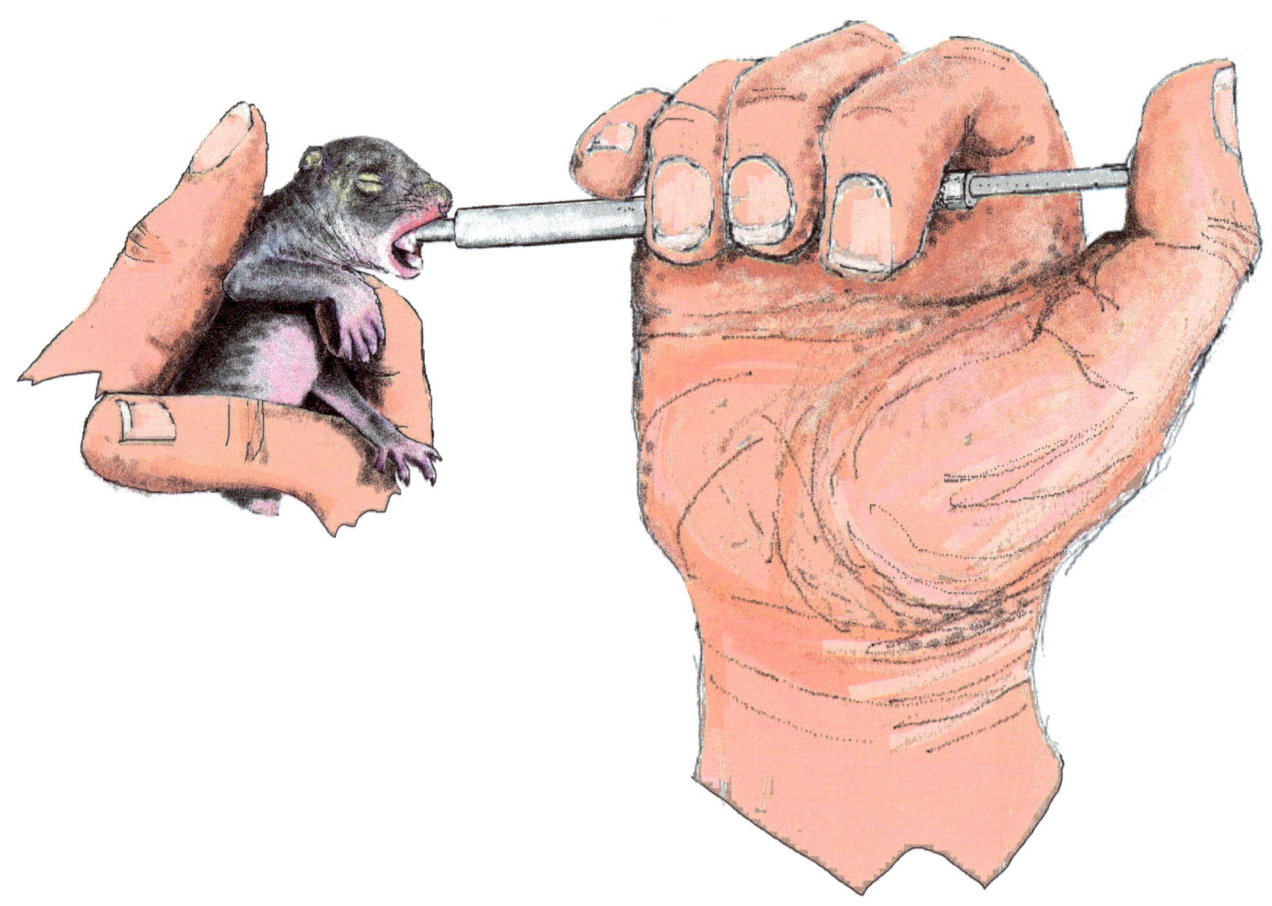

Melissa begged to hold Sally, but Mommy said it wasn't time yet…that stage would come soon enough.

Before too long, Melissa got her wish as Sally entered a new phase of her young life. Mommy had just finished the feeding and had let Melissa hold Sally on her lap while she cleaned the box Sally slept in. Honey, the family's brown and white spotted beagle, made a loud crashing noise outside the room where Sally was being kept. Honey had slid into some toys that Melissa left in the middle of the floor. The loud noise startled Melissa and Sally, and before Melissa even knew what was happening, Sally climbed right up her shirt to the back of her neck and hid under her ponytail. Though her eyes were not yet opened, instinct told her to climb, and that is just what she did!

Melissa could feel a dull stinging pain where Sally's small but sharp claws had scratched the skin on her neck. It didn't hurt much, but she would be more careful next time she was holding Sally and would make sure Honey was contained in a safe place until Sally was safely back in her box. Mommy had cut a hole in one end of the shoebox and put a lid on it. Then she put the box into a medium-sized cage so that Sally would be safe from any intruders…namely, Honey! After each feeding, Sally was tenderly returned to her box, and the door of the cage was locked in place.

Watching the quick growth of Sally was fascinating. Some days, Melissa brought over some of her schoolmates to look in on Sally with her. Not only did Sally seem to grow in size each day, but also her tail fur steadily became fuller and longer. It would twitch and move back and forth depending on how excited Sally was. Her tail went up and down and around and around, and it seemed Sally derived great pleasure from swishing it wildly about while Melissa tried to comb it. Not that it needed to be combed—for Sally had learned by instinct to groom herself—but Melissa loved to comb her baby doll's hair and she was convinced Sally's tail needed the same attention.

Melissa and Mommy were impatient for Sally's eyes to finish forming. It seemed they were never going to open. Then one evening, Melissa noticed a small shiny dot like a black marble staring at her. The first eye had opened! "Hello there, Miss Sally!" Melissa giggled.

By the time Melissa had eaten her dinner and came to watch Sally's next feeding, which happened only four times a day now, Sally's other eye had fully opened. "Yay!" Melissa shouted out. The rest of the family came into the room to see what the noise was all about.

"Yep," Mommy nodded her head when she saw Sally's newest development. "She's ready for the addition of solid food now."

That evening, Melissa put some broken up animal crackers, Cheerios, and bits of an apple into a shallow bowl and left it in the cage. The next morning, there were bits and crumbs all over the clean baby blanket that lined the cage. Mommy and Melissa decided to use newspaper from now on in place of the blanket so that it could be changed often and thrown away.

It was always a good idea to reuse things such as newspaper. The family had always tried to be mindful of conservation and either recycle or reuse as many items as possible. Daddy always said, "We must take care of our world and try to leave it better than we found it." Melissa always thought Daddy was such a smart man. Plus, he was very cuddly, especially whenever she had a bad dream or nightmare, which sometimes happened when she ate too much chocolate or sweets before bedtime or had seen something scary on television.

"Good night, my sweet Sally," Melissa whispered to the growing squirrel each night before climbing into bed. "Good night."

3

Big Day Outside

It was time for Sally to start getting used to the sounds of nature once again. Mommy told Melissa that as soon as Sally was eating solid food, she would spend her days in the outdoor cage. Daddy had built the cage a few years ago for Mommy to use to allow their son Daniel's two ferrets to have some "safe" outdoor time. The cage was taller than Daddy, which he boasted about, so it was six-foot-two. It was just about as big around as a refrigerator and made of wire that was woven together to form small squares. Daddy used heavy-duty wire that had very small squares to make sure a snake could not get in, for they are predators of squirrels and other small animals. Mommy needed to keep all the wildlife safe while in her care. It was perfect for Sally.

Daddy put some large tree limbs that he had collected after a recent storm inside the cage. They were cut to fit just right and stood tall and strong and were perfect for Sally to practice her climbing skills on. Separated from the old tree, the branches no longer produced acorns as they once did. Acorns are one of the foods in a squirrel's

natural diet, though they typically enjoy them while they're still green. Squirrels are very skillful at collecting their food. They can climb a tree 100 feet high and scamper to the end of even the thinnest and softest of branches just to snatch acorns from the tip of the limb.

One time, Melissa was watching two squirrels fighting at the top of a gigantic tree when suddenly both of them fell straight to the ground. She scrunched her eyes closed and drew in a deep breath, afraid to see the squirrels lying on the ground. By the time she worked up the courage to open her eyes, the silly squirrels were running back up the tree to fight some more. And what happened next? They fell to the ground again!

Wow, they must be made of rubber! Melissa thought to herself. Those crazy squirrels fell one more time before they decided enough was enough for one day and went their separate ways.

"Whew," Melissa said aloud, "glad that no one died this time." It does happen, though. Sometimes a fall can break a squirrel's back, and then it cannot move its hind legs; a predator will surely take it as a meal. It can be a sad thing to witness—nature sometimes takes the life of one to feed another…but only the strongest can survive in the wild.

Melissa and Mommy had carefully prepared the cage for Sally before they brought her out. They filled a shallow bowl with a few pieces each of diced apple and pear, grapes (cut in half), broccoli, sweet potato, carrot, squash, and some corn still on the cob. Sally ate many of the same healthy foods that were in Melissa's diet—all of which made for a healthy adult squirrel. Another bowl held nuts, pieces of animal crackers, Cheerios, and acorns that Melissa had picked up around the neighborhood. They even put a few small pinecones in there to help Sally become familiar with some of the natural foods of the area. After being released, she would need to figure out for herself how to chew the pinecones off the tree limbs and then work through the sharp needles to get to the delicious pine nut that is buried deep inside the cone itself. It's not an easy feat!

While she lived in the cage, though, Sally got to be spoiled and have as much food as her little tummy could hold. She would be weaned gradually off the milk formula until she ate only solid food and drank water. Just as any other mammal, squirrels need water, and Sally had a bowl of it in her cage. Wild squirrels can lick dew from a leaf, or they can drink from a creek or lake, or even a puddle formed by rain. Sometimes just the fruit from a tree or new young leaf can provide enough water for the day.

It was Mommy's job to transfer Sally into the outdoor cage, and she needed to make sure there was little chance of Sally getting loose. If that were to happen, she likely would instinctively go straight up a tree the way she had run straight up Melissa's shirt, and all the unfamiliar sounds of the outdoors would frighten her. In that case, she might not come down for a long time. A frightened baby squirrel sitting alone atop a tree would be perfect prey for a hawk, which were plentiful in the area.

So, at last, the big day came, and Sally was released into the outdoor cage. A small handmade wooden box hung from a wire at the back of the cage, and inside it Mommy had placed one of the baby blankets Sally had slept with in the house.

This way, Sally could feel secure experiencing all the sounds of nature while still hiding in the box under the blanket. Thus the old phrase "security blanket!"

As soon as she was placed in the outdoor cage, Sally darted straight to the box prepared for her, just like Mommy said she would. She poked her little face out from time to time to get a quick look around before ducking back inside her safe place. What a cute sight she was!

Mommy and Melissa left Sally outside—she was no longer being coddled like a baby. Now she was beginning her training for adulthood. Mommy and Melissa knew her eventual release would be both a happy and sad event. Sally would soon be back in the wild as nature intended, but it also meant that she would face the dangers that are always only a movement away for a squirrel. This caused Melissa great anxiety, but setting Sally free was the right thing to do!

4

An Emotional Moment

Sally, now three months old, was all furred out from head to tail and no longer needed any milk. She stayed in the outdoor cage day and night. Sally became familiar with the sounds of nature that surrounded her outside, and she climbed without fear all around the inside of the cage, jumping exuberantly from tree limb to tree limb with more energy to spare.

It was time…it was time to set Sally free. Melissa was heartbroken at the thought that Sally might never return, but she had made a promise to Mommy, and now she had to honor it. She knew she would be allowed to call for Sally from time to time and offer her some nuts. *But would Sally decide to come when Melissa called?* Nobody knew the answer to that question. Mommy said if Sally returned at night, they could close the cage to keep her safe just until morning, and then let her out again. *Would Sally choose her box and blanket over a nice tree branch in the wild?* No one knew that answer either.

It was early on a Saturday when the whole family gathered to open the cage door; from now on Sally would be able to come and go as she pleased. Everyone's nerves were tense, but especially Melissa's. Tears rolled down her somber cheeks as she opened the door for Sally to begin her new life in her natural environment…in the world she had seen through metal wires but had not been able to touch.

And Sally did just that. She noticed the clear space that suddenly appeared in the side of her wire cage. At first, she hesitated to move, but then slowly and cautiously made her way outside the cage. With a sudden burst, she jumped onto Melissa's back. Melissa was ready for that and had already put a soft towel over her shoulders…she hadn't forgotten how pointy a squirrel's claws are, even though Sally hadn't meant to cause Melissa any pain the day Honey scared her. Squirrel claws must be sharp to climb tall trees and limbs. They allow squirrels to leap from one branch to another and keep their footing. At times they jump so far they look like they are flying!

Sally sprang from Melissa's shoulder to the outside of the cage, where she held on with her claws, and then she decided to investigate the ground. She sniffed around and played with a dry, dead leaf for a moment, then leapt back onto the cage. Up to the very top of the cage she ran, where the branch of an old oak tree hung low. She immediately jumped to it and ran as fast as she could up the branch to the trunk of the tree. The whole family watched as Sally ran up and down that great oak, stopping only long enough to catch her breath and take in her new surroundings.

Eventually, the family went inside the house, except for Melissa, who sat on the ground and continued to watch Sally investigate the tree with excitement and curiosity. Melissa finally left the tree, but just before dusk, she called for Sally, hoping she could lock her in the cage for the night. Nighttime is a very dangerous time for squirrels. During the day, hawks are circling and catching their meals, but at night there are owls in addition to hawks, plus raccoons and opossums all out hunting for food—and yes, *squirrel* is always on the menu.

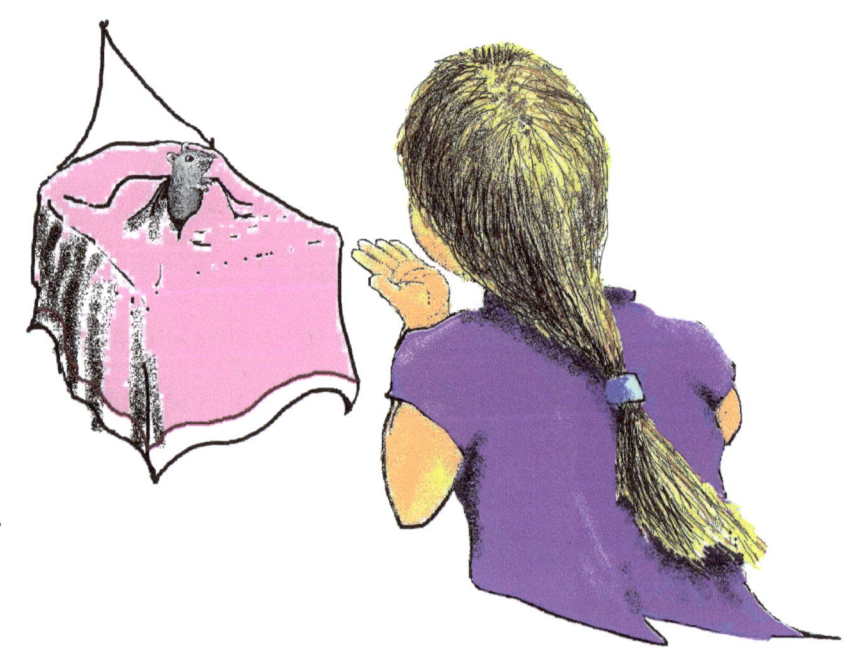

Sally did return this night to the cage, and Melissa shut her inside where she snuggled into the security of her box.

"Good night, Sally!" Melissa said, her fingers curled around the outside of the cage wires. "I love you, and just remember what I taught you. Always look up for hawks and never take chances because you mean a lot to me. You're my best friend, Sally, and you gotta be careful!"

Melissa turned and walked across the yard back to her own habitat—her house—thinking how big the world must seem to such a small animal as a squirrel. She slept well that night knowing Sally was safe and had made it through her first day of freedom.

5

Time to Go

The next few days came and went without a lot of excitement. Sally made it back to her outdoor cage each evening and was safely locked inside for the night.

On the fifth evening after her release, Sally did not return. Melissa tossed and turned all night long with emptiness in her heart, wondering what might have happened to Sally. *Why didn't she return to sleep in the safety of her cage?* Mommy said Sally's natural instincts were guiding her now, and that she had probably already begun to gather leaves, bark, and twigs to build her own nest.

It was hard for Melissa to accept Sally's mysterious absence when she already suffered so many insecurities each day. Most Sunday evenings she would get a sick feeling inside her tummy. Mommy called that feeling "butterflies in the belly," but Melissa knew it as being "homesick"…she knew the next day she would have to leave home for school. She loved being home with Mommy and often felt scared and uncomfortable when she was around a lot of strangers or away from home. Though she did enjoy school once she got there, she was relieved the moment the bell rang, alerting the teachers and students that the school day was finally over.

Sometimes her tummy ached during school, too. She missed her mommy and her animals, her home, and her bedroom. All those things felt safe and orderly. At school she had friends, but she was quiet and did a lot more listening than talking when they played together. Sometimes other children left her out when playing games. But Melissa had a wonderful and active imagination; she loved writing stories and poems, and drawing pictures along with the words. She blushed when she was chosen to read aloud in class and tried very hard to obey all the rules so she would not stick out in the crowd. Her teacher was very fond of her, though, and it pleased Melissa very much to be told she was "such a smart student!"

Though nothing terrible ever happened to Melissa at school, she still counted the minutes until it was time to go home. More fearful of what could happen, rather than what had happened, she tiptoed through each day scanning her world with uncertain eyes—always alert, always on guard. Once she was home, she could relax and play with her toys, and she especially enjoyed taking care of her ever-growing collection of insects and animals.

Mommy had taught her that wildlife could be dangerous and that there were some animals she should never touch or try to catch. Snakes were one of those animals. Mommy taught Melissa and her friends that even though a baby bird, squirrel, or other wildlife may look like they are alone and in need of help, they shouldn't touch them either, because most of the time, the animal's parent could still care for the young one. Sally's case had been special—it was a life or death situation, because she was so cold on the ground by herself that she needed immediate care to avoid dying. Mommy explained that some animal mothers, such as deer, will leave their babies hidden in bushes or tall weeds while they go off to eat and drink, returning to nurse their young fawns with their milk and to cuddle with them to sleep. People sometimes see a fawn and think it's alone and in danger. But the real danger is when a person picks it up and takes it away from its mother—then it has to grow up in a shelter like Sally, without her own kind to teach her. It's better to leave most animals alone, Mommy said, unless they are in imminent danger.

§§§§§

To Melissa and Mommy's delight, the next morning Sally was in the yard running up and down the cage in anticipation of some much-needed food. Though Sally was beginning to forage and find things to eat in her wooded habitat, she still needed some additional nourishment. Eventually, Sally would watch other squirrels and taste-test for herself many different plants, flowers, and seeds. But for now, she returned to eat some of the food that was left outside for her. That is, of course, until the other squirrels in the neighborhood figured out there was free food near the cage each morning.

It was time now for Sally to find her own way in life. Though she came back regularly for treats, she was learning to be a wild squirrel and spent most of the day searching for food, chasing or running away from other squirrels. Sometimes she raced up and down trees just for the fun of it.

For Melissa and her family, the days and weeks went by without any major events. Honey, the family dog, sometimes sneaked out when someone left the front door open too long and did what she did best…chased anything and everything that moved in the yard—which included any squirrel nearby!

The squirrels complained loudly by chattering back in their high-pitched voices. Sally learned to chatter as well, and Melissa could eventually tell Sally's voice from the others. Because she was still so young, her tone was higher than many of the other squirrels. She was learning the ways of the world, and dogs and cats were added to the long list of predators for her to be on guard against. In a squirrel's world, nothing and no place is completely safe—so their instincts, their large eyes, and sensitive hearing are the most important tools they have to help them survive.

Whenever Melissa or Mommy went outside, they carried a handful of pecans, almonds, walnuts, or peanuts to share with Sally and other squirrels and birds that Mommy had raised and released. Most of the time, Sally would show up within minutes and carefully jump onto their clothing, climb to their shoulder, and calmly eat the treats in safety. The other squirrels were more skittish and would only grab the nuts that were thrown on the ground. When Sally heard the alarm calls of the other squirrels, though, she crammed what food she could into her mouth, hopped off their shoulder, and ran to the nearest tree. She reminded Melissa of a bunny hopping across the lawn, but when Sally got to the tree, unlike a bunny, she sprinted right up the tree to the security of a leaf-covered branch and sat frozen until the danger passed.

She was smart, and Mommy and Melissa both knew that if any squirrel could survive in the wild, Sally had a great chance of it.

The paws of a squirrel have four fingers and a small, mostly unusable, thumb, with a soft pad underneath each finger and a long sharp claw at the tip. They are a tree-dwelling animal, which means that, other than foraging on the ground for food, they spend the rest of their time living in the trees, where their sharp claws are a necessity.

§ § § § §

One Sunday morning after church, Melissa began walking toward Sally's favorite tree with her hands full of acorns she had gathered from her neighborhood the previous day. Before she had the chance to call for Sally, the little squirrel was already racing toward her. Melissa was so eager to see Sally that she hadn't even changed out of her white, hard-soled church shoes. It all happened so quickly—Sally raced right under Melissa's foot and she stepped on Sally's long, beautiful tail. Sally sprang forward to get away and left the last two inches of her tail under Melissa's shoe! Melissa quickly backed up, but it was too late—the tip of Sally's tail lay still on the ground and Sally had run away, frightened and injured.

Melissa ran into the house, partial tail in hand. A river of tears fell from her eyes. While Mommy hugged her distraught daughter, she told her all about the amazing tails that squirrels have. Being so long and fluffy, they're perfect for wrapping around themselves like a scarf to keep warm when it's cold. They also are a means of communication. By twitching them in a certain way, they can warn other squirrels of dangers they've spotted nearby. They can even be used as a defense—when being stalked and threatened by a predator, squirrels will shake their tail vigorously, drawing the predator's attention to the quivering fur. The squirrel's strategy is to have his attacker pounce on his tail rather than his body because the tail breaks off fairly easily, which allows the squirrel to escape and live to bury nuts another day. Though the tail does not grow back, it heals quickly, and a squirrel can survive without that part of it.

Melissa was comforted by what she learned and drew her small fingers across her cheeks to wipe away the tears. That night when she went to bed, she picked out a star through her bedroom window and gave it her wish that Sally's tail would be okay.

§ § § § §

Spring had gone, the hot humid summer passed, fall became winter, and soon spring was around the corner once again. As new leaves were sprouting and daytime was becoming longer, it was the hardest time for squirrels. Most of the hidden food had been found or was sprouting into new growth and was no longer good to eat. The best chance the squirrels had to survive was to eat the new sprouts from trees and bushes. Sometimes, if they get hungry enough, squirrels will eat insects and small vertebrae such as lizards and baby birds. Nature will survive any way it can. And Sally, with her tail fully healed, had a little extra help from the snacks Melissa and Mommy put out for her from time to time.

One spring morning, Melissa went outdoors to look for Sally. With a pocketful of nuts, as usual, she called out her name. "Sally! Sally! Sally, where are you?"

The yard was quiet except for the chirping of some nearby birds. She called again, but only silence replied. Melissa called over and over for her beloved Sally. Finally, with a heavy heart and her pockets still bulging with nuts, she went back inside to tell Mommy how lonely she felt.

"Well Honey, there's not much we can do," Mommy said. Melissa felt helpless. "Sally is wild, and though she's smart, many squirrels live short lives. Sometimes they run out of food, and sometimes they are taken by predators. Our own cars are one of their biggest predators…squirrels and other wildlife are often killed by cars and trucks while running across roads as they search for food. It's sad, honey, but it can't be helped."

Melissa hated listening to all the horrible things that could have happened to her Sally. She ran to her room, leaped on her bed and sobbed into her pillow. Mommy came in to comfort her, but Melissa just wanted to be alone. Her thin shoulders shook with anguish. Mommy gave her a gentle kiss on the back of her head and left to start dinner for the family. There was no consoling Melissa right now. Sometimes life hurts, but there is always another day, there are always friends and family, and there is always more to do and more to love. Eventually Melissa would understand all this, but right now, her fears overwhelmed her.

In spite of Sally's absence, Mommy and Melissa still called for her day after day. Sally, it seemed, was nowhere to be found. "I know she's out there somewhere," Melissa comforted herself in whispers. "I know Sally is alive, I just know it!" She had never had such confidence before. She pushed away all her fears of what could *have* happened to Sally. Until she knew what *had* happened, she would remain vigilant in faith.

6

Spring and New Life

Melissa was now in second grade and rode the big yellow school bus home. Each day, she got off the bus and raced inside her house to let Mommy know she was home from school. She would grab a quick snack for herself and fill her pockets with nuts. Then she would go outside and call for Sally.

It had been over a month since she'd been seen—for over a month Melissa had been calling for her every day. Melissa's faith in her survival had finally cracked. Despondent, she called for Sally one last time. Her voice faltered, and once again tears trickled down her soft cheeks for her beloved squirrel—her greatest source of both happiness and heartache. She turned toward the house and took a heavy step…just one. Then her ear caught a familiar noise coming from a low-hanging branch of a nearby tree.

"Sally!" Melissa shouted. "It's Sally!"

Sally moved very slowly down the branch toward Melissa, her hind legs barely moving. The hind legs of squirrels are longer than the forelegs because they do much of the work hanging onto the bark of the trees and limbs. Having little or no use of her hind legs would be a death sentence for Sally, and it was surprising she had made it this far. Sally seemed to be pulling most of her body weight with her front legs. She looked thin and had some wounds on her head, left ear, and her back.

"Oh dear, oh dear!" cried Melissa. She ran to the house and called for Mommy to come quickly. Together they went to the limb Sally had just been on, but found it unoccupied.

Sally was gone. They called out to her for a long time, but either Sally had been snatched up by a predator, or she had gone back to her hiding place. The happy smile that had briefly lit up Melissa's face turned to a frown. Melissa and Mommy went into the house without speaking another word.

It was ten more days before Sally turned up again. Melissa spotted her perched on a high branch near her old nest. She could always tell it was Sally even from far away because of her shorter than normal tail.

Sally looked just about like her old self. She came down the tree head first, which is a specialty trick of a grey squirrel. Melissa kept still as Sally jumped up onto her leg and scampered to her shoulder. Of course, as usual, Melissa had a handful of nuts, for she had never walked outside without hope. She had taken a solitary step away in despair, and it was as if Sally had heard that one hopeless step and knew, in spite of her debilitating injuries, that she needed to let Melissa know she was alive.

Sally was still a little thin, and she ate the nuts hastily. Mommy walked outside to see what was going on. Sally jumped from Melissa's shoulder to Mommy's and back to Melissa's again to finish her treats.

Mommy noticed that Sally's nipples on the underside of her belly were larger than normal and slightly hairless. This was a sign that Sally had given birth in her nest in the spring. But since no babies had ever been seen, and Sally was now out and about, the conclusion was that a predator had gotten to Sally's babies. She had probably tried to save her children, and with that, almost lost her life. A mother animal will do anything to protect her young, even at the cost of her own life. Sally must have been badly hurt and forced to retreat from the fight. By the looks of her injuries, she would never have won that battle, anyway.

Figuring that is what happened, the next day Daddy built a wooden box for Sally. Maybe it would give her a fighting chance to raise some babies of her own when the time was right again. Melissa helped make the box, holding the wood for Daddy as he nailed the pieces of cedar into place. He added a wire mesh to the bottom of the tall box so air could circulate in and any liquid could evaporate or drain through. There was a hole on one side of the box, just big enough for a squirrel to squeeze through. The box was large enough that the squirrel could bring in nesting materials and still be far enough away from the hole that long raccoon arms couldn't reach in and snatch a baby from the nest. Daddy got on a tall ladder and hung it high on the tree that Sally seemed to prefer.

One evening after the box had been mounted onto the tree, Melissa called for Sally and was delighted when her head popped out from the hole that had been designed especially for her.

"Oh, Sally!" Melissa shouted. She pressed her hands together in glee. "You knew this was made for you, didn't you? Good night Sally! Sleep tight."

7

A Special Call for Help

Sally had left her cage in the yard for good, but the yard was far from empty. Mommy had acquired several chickens—twelve hens of several different breeds and one large and very vocal rooster, who had just about every shade of brown and red color throughout his feathers. The hens were a varied group—some were black and white, others were red or black and brown, and one was just plain white. Melissa thought they were a lot of fun to watch as they pecked at the ground to find a bug to eat, or pecked at the young growth of grasses to eat in the backyard. But most amusing of all was to watch them dig ditches in the sandy areas to take a dust bath.

Dust bathing is a behavior that chickens do out of natural instinct. They dig shallow ditches with their feet, roll in the dirt or mulch, scratch it onto their backs, and shuffle it under their feathers. The dirt repels parasites and absorbs excess moisture and oil on their skin and feathers. Sometimes they dig simply in order to rest in cooler soil. After they fling a sufficient amount of dirt, sand, or mulch onto themselves, they shake it all off and then preen and groom their feathers. With all the dirt flying around, it's a

lucky thing chickens have what is considered a third eyelid—in addition to an upper and lower eyelid, they have a membrane between the two which can completely cover their eyeball to protect it. The cornea has its own lubricating duct, kind of like a human's tear duct, which cleans the eye and keeps it moist.

Melissa loved collecting the eggs from the hens' nests in the coop, and whenever her friends or cousins came to visit, she would let them do the collecting. Many times

Mommy would send eggs home with Melissa's friends so they could see how wonderful fresh yard eggs tasted. Mommy researched how to keep pests away by using all natural and organic items, so no harmful chemical pesticides were used around the eggs. It's not so difficult—just a few chores to keep the coop, where the eggs are laid, clean. Mommy also added a little apple cider vinegar in the clean water to help prevent diseases. At the end of the day, she made sure all the uneaten food was put in steel cans so mice, rats, and unwanted insects couldn't get to it at night.

Melissa was sitting on her back porch one afternoon eating a banana Popsicle—her favorite flavor—when she heard a very frantic high-pitched chattering coming from the wooded area nearby. She stood up to get a better view and scanned the backyard area to see if she could spot something out of the ordinary. She saw nothing, but the chattering continued, loud and insistent. And it wasn't just any chattering; Melissa recognized the voice as Sally's.

Melissa got up from her rocking chair and walked closer toward the woods to investigate. There she saw a large hawk trying to eat one of Mommy's chickens! The hawk had landed on the back of one of the black-and-white hens and had already plucked out several of her feathers. Melissa arrived just in time to frighten the hawk, and it flew off without its prey. The chicken was so scared that she just lay there, without a movement, as if she was frozen solid.

Melissa suspected that the poor hen thought she was done for, but Sally's alarm call had saved her.

Melissa picked up the frightened hen and inspected her for any wounds. She had survived the attack without even a scratch to her skin. Then she called in the other chickens for the night. Usually, Mommy did this each night for their safety by calling, "chick, chick, chick," with a handful of scratch in her hand. Melissa didn't have any of this scratch, which was really just cracked corn, seed, and some grains. But the chickens were used to the routine and came in anyway. Melissa locked them all safely inside. As she left the coop, Melissa looked up at the nearest tree, which was where all the chattering had come from. There sat Sally, close to the trunk, her tail still flicking up and down.

"Thank you, Sally. Thank you so much! I love you."

That night Melissa said a special prayer for Sally and all the chickens in her backyard. "Please, God, keep Sally safe, and thank you for bringing her to our family."

News travels fast in school, and the children in Melissa's class soon learned all about Sally's heroic act—saving the family's hen from a hawk. Melissa's teacher had given a class assignment in which each student was to write an essay about someone or something that brought them joy and happiness. Melissa, of course, wrote the story of Sally—how she was rescued and eventually released back into the wild. She finished her paper with this:

Sally makes me smile. When I see her so high up in a tree, or hiding a nut or seed in the soil, then burying and covering it up so carefully with nearby leaves and twigs, I smile. To me, Sally is nature, and I believe that nature is so beautiful. I know someday Sally will not come back when I call, but I am willing to bear with that sadness just to know she has lived her life the way it was meant for her to. That makes me happy.

8

Age Takes a Toll

Life went on, and Sally wasn't the only one getting older. Melissa had turned fourteen and entered the ninth grade. Her high school years had begun, which she would find to be a very busy four years of her life. As for Sally, a squirrel's lifespan, and that of many other animals, is shorter than that of humans. Melissa was still young and had the prime of her life ahead of her, but Sally was becoming a rather elderly little squirrel.

Sally had lost another part of her beautiful tail during some kind of altercation and now could be spotted easily, even from far away, because of her stubby tail. Sally also gained a slight dark line on both sides of her cheeks. Otherwise, she looked nearly the same, but though she was ever cautious in the woods, there was a growing slowness in her movements. There was no doubt how smart and intuitive Sally was. The proof was how long she had stayed alive and thrived in her woods.

Over the years, Sally had given birth to a litter of babies in the house that Daddy had made for her high up in a nearby tree. She eventually made a new home in a tree with a good size hole in its trunk. She had her second litter there. Melissa watched with amazement when the new babies (fully furred out) peeked out of the entrance hole in the tree to have a look at the big world outside. Sometimes they ventured out and ran up and down the tree, staying close to the nest in case a predator was near. Sally had three babies in each litter, and Melissa thought they were the cutest things ever! One time when Melissa went to the tree, all three babies had their tiny heads sticking out of the hole they used to enter and exit.

Their eyes were big, round, and dark. Melissa always thought the eyes of squirrels were so beautiful, just like the eyes of a deer—they looked so innocent and sweet. Sight is one of the squirrel's most important senses, and a pointy stick or another squirrel's claw during a fight can injure their eyes. A one-eyed squirrel doesn't usually make it very long in the wild. Their vision is extremely important; they rely on it to spot danger and stay clear of it.

Melissa was gone from her house more and more, but the children in the neighborhood and from school always asked about Sally, and they often dropped by to call Sally in from the woods to give her some nuts they had brought from home. Sally was well known now, and Mommy shared a lot of her knowledge about wildlife to children since she was now a volunteer and foster parent at a nearby wildlife sanctuary. Sometimes the director, Dorothy, or one of the assistant directors, Cheryl or Karen, would call and ask Mommy to foster a few new arrivals to the sanctuary. Much of the time they were baby squirrels, bunnies, ducks, or opossums. She would remind everyone who visited their home about the need to spay and neuter their pets—especially cats, because they multiply so fast and are our wildlife's worst enemy.

Mommy and Melissa started a neighborhood recycling effort, and it went quite well, with at least half the neighbors showing effort in reusing items to avoid increasing the size of dangerous landfills. Whether she realized it or not, Melissa had been growing into a strong and independent young lady. After spending years exploring nature, collecting bugs, helping to raise and release various animals, Melissa had learned some hard lessons in life, as some of the rescued animals and pets died from time to time.

This was never easy for Melissa or Mommy, but knowing they did the best they could for the animals helped them recover from the grief they felt. There was always another animal in need, and as time went on, Melissa grew to see that life goes on even when we feel the pain and loss of a loved one. We must be grateful for the time and love that was exchanged, and celebrate that.

Melissa played the saxophone in the school band and was often busy practicing at school or playing in the band at ball games, and she was involved in several school functions. If she got home in time before nightfall, she called for Sally even after so many years had passed. She always brought some peanuts or pecans, which were Sally's all-time favorites.

As Mommy and Melissa always knew and secretly dreaded, there came a time when Sally did not show up for several weeks after being called. It was winter and devastatingly cold that year. It was a sharp change from the mild winters that were the norm. Melissa feared the worst about Sally. Night after night, one of the family members called for her and left nuts under the trees where Sally would normally be found resting. Her tree house that Daddy had built had long been taken over by another squirrel, younger and more vivacious than Sally. She had also been pushed out of the nest she had built inside the tree with a hole in its trunk. Sally had another nest out in the woods now.

Days went by and the weather got colder and colder, and everyone imagined Sally was not faring well. Without a long fuzzy tail to keep her warm in her old age, she didn't stand much of a chance in such a bitter winter.

One evening, Mommy asked Melissa to put the chickens up for the night and bring in the eggs that had been laid that day. As she collected the eggs—which totaled ten large brown ones and two white ones—she spotted a squirrel sitting on the lowest limb of a nearby bush. The bush was barren of leaves so she could see it was her Sally. Melissa almost dropped all the eggs on the ground as she rushed over to where Sally rested. She put the basket of eggs down, and Sally left the branch, stopping just short of Melissa's leg. She was weak and thin and had lost much of her fur on the lower part of her back. It was possibly the result of frostbite. Melissa knew Sally couldn't make it in the frigid cold—the temperature was going down to about eighteen degrees that night. Melissa was wearing a long tee-shirt and before Sally knew it, Melissa had picked her up from the ground and covered her with the front part of her shirt, holding her close to her warm belly, very much like the day she picked up the little pink baby and brought her home. She wasn't at all worried about being bitten by Sally, because not only was Sally always very gentle, but also squirrels don't usually carry diseases such as rabies and distemper like some other wildlife do. Though there was always a chance of being bitten by any of the other animals that were raised and released, Sally had not once bitten anyone.

Melissa felt Sally's cool body and rushed inside the house to warm her. She found the old cage that was used as Sally's first home outside her mother's nest. She turned the heating pad on and then she locked the cage. Melissa brought some fresh water and food into the cage and Sally started to eat right away. Of course, she chose the pecans first!

Daddy offered to bring in the outdoor cage and put it in Melissa's room so she could take care of Sally through the harsh winter. The intention was to assist Sally through this tough time and release her again in the spring. The family knew that Sally, once again, had managed to survive some kind of trauma, but everyone also knew that she had lived past the average expected lifespan of a wild squirrel. Every day with her was a blessing.

Melissa was so happy to see Sally comfortable and warm in her swinging bed. Melissa would close her bedroom door and open the cage so Sally could run around the room. She looked out the windows, and sometimes she chattered when she heard other squirrels chattering outside. Melissa enjoyed their time together and loved it when Sally sat perched on a tree limb that Daddy cut for Sally to climb. Sally's eyes were so big, and they held so much knowledge and love, and probably also some grief. Melissa found those deep eyes so precious, and she loved Sally with every ounce of her heart.

§ § § § §

Spring was around the corner, and Sally had made good progress under Mommy's constant supervision and was ready to be set free once again. Melissa and Mommy petted Sally on the head, then took her to the nearest tree outside and released her. Sally ran up the tree and sat on a branch. She looked down at Melissa, and Melissa looked up at her. There was a bond between them that could never be broken.

Just as Sally had grown up and become independent and strong, Melissa had also found a new independence and she became more outgoing with her friends. She dealt with the ups as well as the downs that life threw her from time to time. She felt that all the discoveries she made while caring for the animals had shaped her into the strong and confident young lady she was now. Sally had played a big part in her growth, and Melissa knew it. In witnessing Sally's strength and resilience to the harsh realities of life in the wild, Melissa's eyes were opened to all the possibilities that life holds, and her heart learned the value and rewards of hope and optimism.

Sally's sanctuary was a place called the woods—a place where she could be wild and free. Melissa called a house her sanctuary—the place where she felt secure and happy with her family and her animals. But no matter what someone names it, we all need one. We all need a sanctuary, a place we can call home.

About the Author

Doreen (Claiborne) Ingram's deep love for animals led her to write her first book to support some very special chimpanzees living in a sanctuary in South Africa. From then on, she made it her goal to spread the word about the distressing plight of all great apes and other endangered wildlife.

She visits wildlife sanctuaries, volunteering whenever possible, to gain firsthand knowledge of a wide variety of animals. With this knowledge and experience, she speaks at schools, libraries, and other venues, teaching both children and adults about wildlife and the sanctuaries that help them, sharing and spreading her empathy for the animals. Additionally, Doreen shares the net profits from the sale of her books and games and from venue presentations with the sanctuaries and organizations that help rescue and house animals in need.

The Illustrator

Illustrator—Mark Ingram. This is Mark's first venture at illustration in support of sister-in-law Doreen's empathy for the courageous animal. When he is not doing this, he enjoys what blessed life brings with his wife, Teresa, and their faithful Labrador, Pearl. SEMPER FIDELIS.

Mark is very appreciative of Doreen's hard work and thanks her for everything she does for animals. This illustration reflects this book and the previous books she has authored.

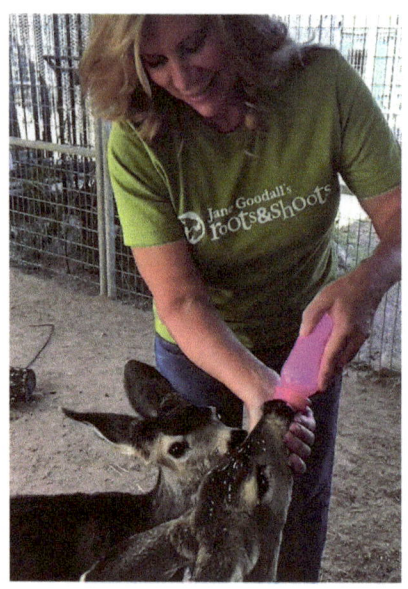

Feeding the baby deer.

Fostering baby squirrels until time for their release.

THIS IS SALLY!

Doreen volunteering at Keepers of the Wild Sanctuary.

Doreen with her hero, Dr. Jane Goodall.

www.doreeningram.com

www.ingramcontent.com/pod-product-compliance
Lightning Source LLC
Chambersburg PA
CBHW061145010526
44118CB00026B/2882